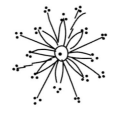

THE CROSBY GARRETT HELMET

Edited by

D J Breeze and M C Bishop

with a Foreword by

R Cooke

an Introduction by

D Ekserdjian

and with contributions by

M C Bishop, D Boughton, D Bradbury, D J Breeze,
J C N Coulston, M Graham, C Healey, and P Shaw

THE ARMATVRA PRESS

Published by

The Armatura Press
39–41 High Street
Pewsey
Wiltshire SN9 5AF
UK

thearmaturapress.co.uk

for

Tullie House Museum & Art Gallery
Castle Street
Carlisle
Cumbria CA3 8TP
UK

www.tulliehouse.co.uk

Typeset by M C Bishop at The Armatura Press

ISBN 978-0-9570261-7-9

Printed in England by Wessex Print Centre

Cover photos: the restored Crosby Garrett helmet (© Christie's Images Limited [2010])

CONTENTS

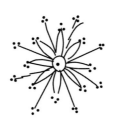

FOREWORD

The recent discovery of the Crosby Garrett Roman Helmet in a field above the Eden Valley, some 20 miles south of Carlisle, can already be seen as a key event in the development of our understanding of Roman life and culture. Moreover the Helmet itself is one of the great masterpieces of Roman metalwork – unparalleled in its detail and the most complete and elaborate of only three such helmets to have been found in Britain. We were therefore delighted that Tullie House Museum was selected to mount the first public exhibition to focus specifically on this magnificent bronze object. We were honoured to have been asked to do this in partnership with the British Museum, where the helmet will be exhibited early in 2014, after its three months with us.

We are also delighted to have been able to commission this publication, which accompanies the exhibition. Both exhibition and publication are separate but related parts of a single project that brings the Helmet to life after almost two thousand years. Of the several parties who have been involved in enabling this project to happen, our thanks go first and foremost to the owner of the Crosby Garrett Roman Helmet, both for his generosity in lending the Helmet to us, which has enabled it to be put on display to the public in the part of the world where it was found, and for supporting this publication.

We also wish to thank:

- Professor David Breeze, Dr Mike Bishop and the authors of the different sections of this publication – Professor David Ekserdjian, Dot Boughton, Mark Graham, Trish Stewart, Chris Healey and Jon Coulston. We particularly wish to thank David Breeze for planning and editing this publication.
- Museum Het Valkhof, Nijmegen, and National Museums Scotland, which have provided images for this publication.
- Roger Bland, Keeper in the Departments of Prehistory and Europe and Portable Antiquities and Treasure, Helen Parkin, Loans Administrator in the Department of Prehistory and Europe, and Ralph Jackson, Curator of Romano-British Collections, all of the British Museum for helping with the arrangements.
- The Monument Trust, The Art Fund, The Friends of Tullie House and Carlisle City Council for funding the exhibition that accompanies this publication.
- Tim Padley, Curator of Archaeology, and Andrew Mackay, Head of Collections and Programming at Tullie House, who were responsible for curating the exhibition.
- Professor David Ekserdjian and Judith Nugee, both of whom provided invaluable advice and assistance at various critical stages during the gestation of this project.

Lastly, I must record our appreciation of the unstinting energy and commitment of our Director, Hilary Wade, who has managed the numerous administrative, logistical, financial and legal aspects involved in organising this important exhibition.

Roger Cooke
Chairman, Tullie House Museum and Art Gallery Trust, Carlisle

PREFACE

David J Breeze and M C Bishop

The Crosby Garrett helmet is a remarkable find. This amazing object was discovered by metal detectorists on the fells high above the River Eden in Cumbria, the territory nearly 2,000 years ago of the Carvetii, a self-governing region within the Roman province of Britain. Its find-spot lies nearly 10km from the nearest Roman fort of Brough on the Stainmore Pass. Since its discovery, archaeologists have been finding out more about its location.

The first step was to undertake a geophysical survey of the area around the find-spot to see if any archaeological features were revealed: they were. The second was to undertake a limited excavation to examine the find-spot itself in order to seek to understand the context of the helmet better. Both actions produced helpful results and these are discussed in this booklet. In short, the helmet lay in an area of settlement, presumably a farm, occupied by the indigenous people of Britain. But why the helmet was buried there is a question we may never be able to answer. In the meantime, the survey and excavation have demonstrated the need to understand better both rural settlements in northern England during the Roman period and the interaction between these people and the Roman army and Roman officials.

This work could not have been undertaken without the agreement of Eric Robinson of Crosby Garrett and we are most grateful to him for that, for the financial support of the Portable Antiquities Scheme, based at the British Museum, and to Roger Bland for facilitating this help. We are also grateful to many friends in Britain and abroad who have helped to produce this booklet in double-quick time, not least through the production of illustrations. Our final thanks go to Christie's who allowed analysis of the metal in the helmet, discussed below, and facilitated the provision of information and photographs for use in this booklet and for archaeologists generally.

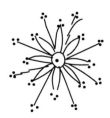

INTRODUCTION

David Ekserdjian

The Crosby Garrett Helmet is without question one of the most spectacular archaeological finds of recent years. Excavated at Crosby Garrett in Cumbria as recently as May 2010, it was then the star lot of Christie's Antiquities sale at King Street a few months later on 7 October of the same year, where it was acquired by a private collector. Now, it will be the focus of an exhibition at the Tullie House Museum from 30 October 2013 to 27 January 2014, of which the present publication is the catalogue.

This is the second time it has been displayed in public since its appearance at auction. In the autumn of 2012, it was one of the absolute stars of the *Bronze* exhibition at the Royal Academy, of which I was one of the organisers. In that context, it was part of a large-scale and global survey of bronze sculpture from its origins in the fourth millennium BCE to the present, and found itself in the company of major pieces from the Middle East, Asia, and Africa. Thanks above all to the enthusiasm for the project of numerous lenders, both public and private, a particular strength of that show were the Greek and Roman antiquities, and the Crosby Garrett Helmet was not the only recent discovery. On the contrary, it kept company with the *Dancing Satyr* from Mazara del Vallo, which was fished out of the sea in 1998, and the *Portrait Head of King Seuthes III* from Sofia, which was found in the Golyama Kosmatka tumulus in the vicinity of the town of Shipka in central Bulgaria in 2004.

All three finds underline one of the most exciting aspects of the study of the history of art, namely the fact that the most extraordinary masterpieces continue to be added to the canon. Unsurprisingly, many of these – one thinks of the *Bronzes of Riace* or the whole array of treasures found in the tomb of Phillip of Macedon at Vergina – are the results of underwater explorations or archaeological digs, but others date from far more recent times, and are not. In the context of renaissance and later art, the works in question have often – although not invariably – been published in the past under less illustrious names, and as copies or imitations of the productions of the greatest masters. Raphael's *Madonna of the Pinks*, which re-emerged in 1992, is arguably the most celebrated case in point of recent decades, but it is by no means unique. On both flanks, so to speak, all bets are off concerning what 'wonderful things' – to borrow Howard Carter's phrase – may be waiting to take a bow, and to perform an almost miraculous act of benign sabotage to our cherished notions concerning the art of the past. As I write, the current (October 2013) issue of the *Burlington Magazine* features an article on a major new painting by Titian of the *Resurrection of Christ*. Whenever one reads a news report of a newly discovered sonnet by Shakespeare or sonata by Mozart, it almost invariably and virtually instantly transpires that it is nothing of the kind. Only in the context of the visual arts do the objects themselves – on occasion at least – live up to the headlines.

The lion's share of this catalogue is devoted to the most up-to-the-minute archaeological study of the Crosby Garrett Helmet. At the same time, the Helmet is a hauntingly unforgettable work of art. It does not need to be seen or thought of as one thing or the other, because it is so obviously both. No doubt most individual visitors will be marginally more captivated by either its history or its beauty, but it is hard to imagine any of them being left unmoved by its extraordinary presence and power.

DESCRIPTION

M C Bishop

The Crosby Garrett helmet is of a type known as a Roman cavalry 'sports' helmet, made for use in a form of mock combat known as the *hippika gymnasia* (see below). It was never intended as a battle helmet although, as will become apparent, it was still necessary for it to provide the wearer with some degree of practical protection.

There are two principal components to the 407mm-high helmet: the bowl, covering the top, sides, and rear of the wearer's head, and a mask modelled to resemble a human face (Figures 1–10). The rear half was designed to overlap the front and both components, which were hinged together at the top, were fashioned as single pieces of copper alloy, with the area of the face tinned. Examination with a portable X-ray fluorescence spectrometer produced average results of 82% copper, 10% zinc, and 8% tin (Worrell *et al* 2011), indicative of a tin brass.

The face mask, in common with all such helmets, is disturbingly expressionless. At first glance, the most striking element is the pierced eyes, designed so that the rider had sufficient vision whilst mounted to allow for control of his horse and accurate aiming of weapons. Each eye incorporates a pierced circle to suggest the iris and the pupil, a feature which helps to indicate a likely date for the helmet. Incised strokes on the lids of both eyes are used to represent eyelashes. Gracefully arching eyebrows are modelled as narrow ridges of raised, inward-pointing chevrons, rather than realistically rendered. The nose is delicate, has pierced nostrils, and has been dented at the tip before deposition. A pursed, slightly protuberant mouth completes the face which has a fleshy, youthful appearance. The lips are parted, separated by a horizontal slit with a circular expansion at either end. The face mask is framed to the top and either side by three rows of luxurious, yet stylised, curls of hair. These conceal the ears that are often an emphasised component of such face masks. Below the position of the ears, near the rear lower corners of the face mask, are the remains of ferrous studs, used for securing the front and rear halves of the helmet by means of a strap or straps. Taken together, the features appear markedly feminine, which is unsurprising amongst cavalry sports helmets.

The helmet bowl, rather than imitating hair as was so often the case with sports helmets, rises to a forward-pointing, rounded peak typical of a Phrygian cap. The Romanised oriental god Mithras was often depicted wearing a similar piece of headgear. A cast figurine of a griffin – a mythical winged and beaked creature – has been soldered to the top of the helmet (Figure 10). Its fur is suggested by incised, upward-pointing arrows on the body and parallel incisions behind its legs and on the ruff around its neck, whilst the feathers of its raised wings are similarly incised. There is a loop behind the neck of the creature, which is depicted seated, with its front right paw resting upon a two-handled vessel with a flared base (a *kantharos*). Below the *kantharos*, which is decorated with incised arcading, is a concave, oval setting for a jewel or glass-paste gem, now missing. That in turn sits above another loop. Although the griffin appears like an afterthought, perched atop the peak of the Phrygian cap, the incorporation of the jewel (found on other, similar helmets) suggests it was always envisaged as part of the original design and may have served to support a

Figure 1: The Crosby Garrett helmet (front) (© Christie's Images Limited [2010])

Figure 2: The Crosby Garrett helmet (rear) (© Christie's Images Limited [2010])

Figure 3: The Crosby Garrett helmet (front right) (© Christie's Images Limited [2010])

Figure 4: The Crosby Garrett helmet (front left) (© Christie's Images Limited [2010])

Figure 5: The Crosby Garrett helmet (detail of incised pattern on the rear of the bowl)
(© Christie's Images Limited [2010])

front-to-back crest box. Examination of the griffin with the portable X-ray fluorescence spectrometer showed it to have been a leaded bronze with 68% copper, 18% tin, 10% lead, and 4% zinc (Worrell 2011).

The front rim of the bowl has been finished with a raised cable design, edged with incised arcading on the main body of the bowl. At the top, and in the centre of the rim, a hinge was attached to the underside of the bowl by means of two circular rivets, each decorated with three incised concentric rings. Traces of the ferrous pin were apparent during conservation. A corresponding slot in the rim of the face mask engaged with this hinge to join the two halves, which could then be secured using the straps described above. Nearby on the rim, a patch had been applied, in the form of a rectangular piece of sheet metal folded over (and shaped to) the rim and secured with two rivets, in order to repair a crack in the bowl (Figure 6).

The rear of the bowl has a small, almost residual neck-guard, the edge of which has been rolled downwards, presumably partly for reinforcement. It is pierced by a central rivet hole, punched through from the upper surface, since it is slightly dished. There are two other such holes, one on either side, near the front angles of the neck-guard (rivet holes were normally punched, rather than drilled, on Roman helmets). These were probably part of the original means of fastening the two

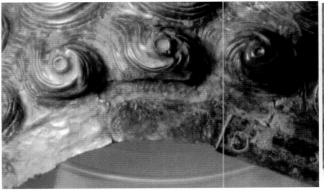 

Figure 6: The hinge slot in the mask (centre) with the riveted patch (right) (© Darren Bradbury)

Figure 7: The four nicks at the junction of the neck-guard and bowl (© Darren Bradbury)

halves of the helmet, together with the ferrous studs on the face mask. Underneath the neck-guard, at the junction with the helmet bowl, there are four nicks (Figure 7). The purpose of these is unknown, but they may have helped match bowl to mask (pairing marks being common on items of cavalry harness such as pendants and decorative discs, or *phalerae*).

Above the neck-guard, around the occipital region, there is a raised ridge which continues round to the front and terminates on either side within an upward-curving volute, just short of the front edge of the bowl. The ridge is decorated with moulded egg and dart motifs on its upper and lower surfaces, with moulded beading along the centre. It is again edged with incised arcading, above and below, on the bowl surface. There are also two small, cast loops fixed to it, the one on the right-hand side still retaining a ring. It is possible that the loops on the griffin ornament may also have been intended for similar rings. Beneath the ridge is a single incongruous row of stylised, raised curls. It is unclear whether this was intended to represent hair protruding from the rear of the Phrygian cap or was simply a decorative flourish.

At the centre of the rear of the bowl there is an intriguing little incised motif, in the form of an eight-petalled flower. Each petal is accompanied by three dots near its tip, and interspersed with three fine tendrils, each longer than the petals and similarly terminated with three dots. Smaller versions of the motif occur on either side of the bowl, above the volutes, and on either side of the griffin (Figure 10).

No plume tubes were present, but that does not mean they could not originally have been soldered in place and subsequently removed. Attachment of such accessories was not always accomplished using rivets. The function of the rings around the back of the bowl is unclear but may relate to a secondary fastening system, replacing the original one, which is now only marked by the three punched holes in the neck-guard. The purpose of the two loops on the griffin ornament is unknown but may have related to the crest box attachment.

There have been three significant studies of cavalry 'sports' helmets, all producing slightly differing typologies, but it is clear that the Crosby Garrett helmet belongs within Type E of Robinson's (1975) classification, it is a Type VI according to Kohlert (1978), and is an example of the Straubing type of Born and Junkelmann (1997). Three types of warrior from the Trojan War (as described in

13

Figure 8: The Crosby Garrett helmet (right side) (© Christie's Images Limited [2010])

Figure 9: The Crosby Garrett helmet (left side) (© Christie's Images Limited [2010])

Figure 10: The Crosby Garrett helmet (details of the griffin ornament)
(© Christie's Images Limited [2010])

the *Iliad* and the *Odyssey* and, in the Roman period, in the *Aeneid*) were depicted by such helmets: Trojans, Amazons, and Greeks. Given the depiction of the Phrygian cap, the helmet is almost certainly intended to depict the first of these. Comparison with other such helmets, and a consideration of the broader context of the piece, can be found in greater detail below.

DISCOVERY

Dot Boughton

The Crosby Garrett 'sports' helmet was discovered by two metal detectorists in May 2010 in Cumbria. They recovered it damaged and broken into several dozen fragments with only the face mask and the lower rim of the head piece still intact. After its discovery it was almost immediately taken to London where it was restored and sold to an anonymous buyer at Christie's antiquities sale on 7 October of the same year.

The finders, a young man and his father from County Durham, had enjoyed detecting in Cumbria for quite some time before the discovery of the helmet even though the fields near Crosby Garrett had never yielded any exciting finds or Treasure (as defined by the Treasure Act of 1996). When taken to the find-spot by the two finders, my colleague and I were told how many countless hours it took to find even one Roman coin in this area – and that the few finds were usually scattered over a huge area. Very rarely would one field yield more than one or two prehistoric or Roman finds. The helmet does fit this description, too, in some ways in that the finder told us that nothing else had been found with it. The helmet was discovered with the nearly unscathed visor face-down in the ground, and the back of the helmet broken off but folded and deposited inside the visor. There were at least 68 other fragments but they, too, lay close by and nothing pointed to, for example, the helmet having been part of a hoard or a human burial (Figures 11–12).

Unfortunately, the helmet itself could not be analysed in detail before the sale (Figures 11–16). Analysis of the metal, however, was undertaken by Ruth Fillery-Travis (2011) using a portable X-ray fluorescence spectrometer. In total, 26 separate analyses were conducted, which indicated that the average results for various parts of the helmet were 82% copper, 10% zinc and 8% tin. The helmet and face appear to have been made from scrap metals, including brass. The griffin mount had been cast from a completely different alloy than the face or helmet, similar in com-

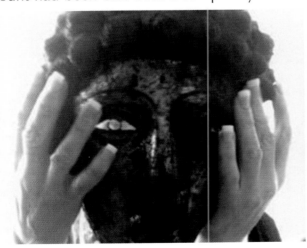

Figure 11: Mobile phone photo of the face mask when found (© finder)

Figure 12: Mobile phone photo of the griffin ornament when found (© finder)

17

Figure 13: The Crosby Garrett helmet mask during restoration (© PAS)

position to Romano-British mirrors. The visor retains traces of tin on the surface which would have given the face a silvering effect. The helmet would therefore have been a striking combination of shiny silver (the visor) and coppery-gold (the helmet). It comes as no surprise that objects like these are very rare discoveries and it is quite possible that another century will pass before another helmet of this splendour is found in Britain.

Figure 14: The Crosby Garrett helmet bowl during restoration (© PAS)

RESTORATION

Darren Bradbury

I spent some 240 hours on a complex and delicate restoration project. My goal was to prepare the mask (visor) and helmet for display, but not to overrestore them. Traces of cracks and splits can still be seen, and the lightly cleaned surfaces retain some earth. The repairs can be reversed.

I closed cracks by hand, using pliers and small clamps covered with masking tape to protect the patina; I also worked the more damaged helmet with shaping hammers and dollies, used as lightly as possible. I tacked cracks and joins together with cyanoacrylate and reinforced them internally with resin, which I sanded smooth and then textured to match the inner surfaces. I took a silicon mould from the mask's hair to cast a resin section of about one-and-a-half missing locks, and I similarly filled a hole in the chin some 5–6cm across, oil-gilding the resin with silver leaf and distressing it. The majority of external joins were filled and touched in accordingly to match the surface patina. I resinned the griffin into place at the top (where lead remains indicated the original fixing).

The mask and helmet had been joined by a simple hinge at the centre of the upper rim, attached by two decorated rivets. Powdery deposits of iron oxide indicated the former iron hinge pin. Ancient wear marks can be seen on the mask's upper rim, caused by opening and closing the helmet. An ancient repair consisting of a piece of bronze sheet had been folded over the mask rim near the hinge, and riveted into place to stabilise two splits, possibly from the time of manufacture.

Figure 15: The Crosby Garrett helmet griffin ornament during restoration (© PAS)

Figure 16: The Crosby Garrett helmet before restoration (© Christie's)

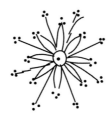

GEOPHYSICAL AND LANDSCAPE SURVEY

Mark Graham and Patricia Shaw

Introduction

Grampus Heritage and Training Ltd conducted a geophysical survey on land close to Crosby Garrett, Cumbria, following the discovery of the helmet. The investigation sought, by means of geophysical and landscape survey, to detect and record surviving archaeological features and anomalies, in the immediate surrounding area of the find-spot. This was to assess the archaeological context of the discovery, and so determine whether the find was associated with an archaeological site. A brief topographic survey was also carried out to detect any extant features close to where the helmet had been recovered.

The Geophysical and Landscape surveys

Fieldwork took place over four days in December 2011. Adverse weather conditions at times affected the tight schedule! The fieldwork began by accurately measuring out a 20 by 20m grid across the area to be surveyed. A magnetometer was then used methodically across this grid to measure and record variations in the magnetic field. This results in a 'greyscale plot', where the more positive the strength of the magnetic field, the darker the image seen in that area of the plot; the more negative the magnetic field, the lighter the image (Figure 17).

The final results were accurately referenced within Ordnance Survey map data using an electronic measuring device (Leica TCR 307) to plot the grid position in association with field boundaries. From this plot archaeological anomalies were detected and some theoretically interpreted, although the intensity of detected anomalies means that not all anomalies could be explained here.

The geophysical survey results revealed a clear area of archaeological activity close to where the helmet was found. A rectilinear structure, curving lines of possible pits, and earthworks, were already visibly noted in the field. In addition to these, several other archaeological anomalies were visible in the data including linear boundaries, small enclosures, hut circles and areas of strong magnetic disturbance that could indicate industrial activity or burning. A concentration of archaeological activity was recorded towards the centre north of the survey area.

A brief landscape survey was conducted in the immediate area around the find-spot, in order to place the survey location and find-spot within a broader landscape context. Field observations recorded a substantial bank and ditch earthwork; a possible defended entrance in the outer boundary; a hut circle earthwork; and a possible settlement enclosure to the west of the survey area. The results of the survey seen in Figure 18 clearly demonstrated that the helmet was deposited within an archaeological context.

Forming a striking feature in the landscape, the large bank and ditch earthwork still defines the extent of enclosed land to the south of the survey area, and can be seen in Figure 18. The line of

Key

Archaeological
Anomaly

Traverses missed out due
to steep terrace slope.

0   20   40   60   80   100   Meters

Figure 17: Results of geophysical survey

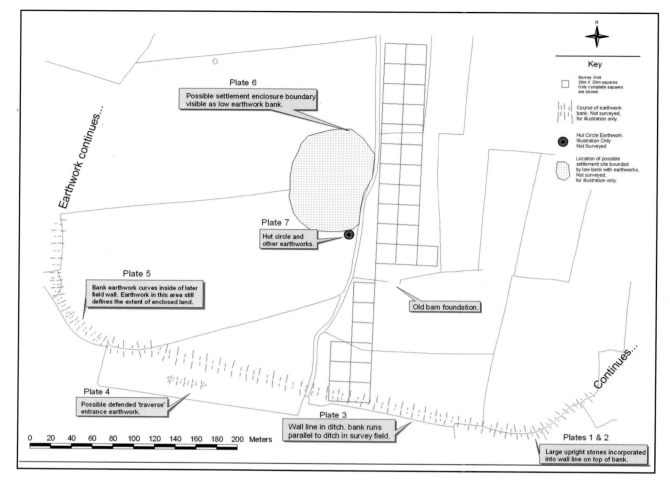

Figure 18: Results of landscape survey

this earthwork has subsequently been closely followed by later field walls. Common land and open fell lie beyond the earthwork to the south. This may be evidence of an ancient enclosure boundary, the full extent of which could not be traced at the time.

The earthwork is most prominent in the field to the south-west of the survey area, crossing an open field, where there is a small section of double bank. Continuing down the southern side of the surveyed area, a later field wall was constructed in the ditch of the earthwork, whilst to the south-east the bank was seen to continue with a later field wall built on top of it. Several large upright stones of an earlier boundary, perhaps contemporary with the earthwork, were noted in this area.

To the bottom left, Figure 18 shows the short section of double bank, where the main earthwork is broad and snaking, contrasting with the short section of offset bank, that appears very straight and narrower than the main earthwork. This straight bank has strong parallels with the style of traverse which helped to defend the entrances of Roman camps, creating a double defence, each earthwork offset to the other. The main earthwork is, however, uncharacteristic of Roman defensive structures.

Plate 1

Plate 2

Plate 3

Plate 4

Plate 5

Plate 6

Plate 7

Plate 8

The probability is that the straight external defensive bank is a later addition to the earthwork. This is possibly a Romano-British adoption of a Roman defensive technique intended to strengthen an Iron Age earthwork in that section.

Immediately to the west of the survey area, archaeological earthworks were seen that included one defined hut circle, to the north of which lay a low bank which appeared to curve. Possibly the boundary enclosure for an Iron Age or Romano-British settlement, this site has not been surveyed. The landowner informed us that Roman coins had been found in this area.

The rectilinear and curvilinear anomalies seen in the middle left section of Figure 17, clearly archaeological, corresponded to earthworks visible on the ground in the west of the survey area. They show a negative white outline, possibly from wall foundations, and appear to enclose an area of darker positive magnetic disturbance, indicating more archaeological features. A dark linear anomaly appears to join the feature. This curvilinear feature relates to a visible earthwork showing as a curved bank, a linear section is adjoined and defined by a curved shallow arc.

To the north-east of this, a strong, broad curving area of positive readings, resulting from features within the visible bank, possibly pits or postholes, can be seen. Other archaeological linear features, both straight and curved, show in Figure 17, possibly representing a sequence of small enclosures and field boundaries. One of these straight linear anomalies was visible in the field as a short length of bank or wall base.

At the northern-most region of the survey area, located on level terrain to the north of a relict dry-stone field wall, four possible hut circles can be seen in Figure 18. Two strongly magnetic linear anomalies, showing as black and white, are archaeological features. The strong variation in the features probably relates to industrial activity of unknown date, as it means the recorded data shows a great difference in magnetism, seen as black for positive and white for negative.

The survey grid, extended further south to include the highest area of ground in the survey site, included land lying close to the large bank and ditch earthwork illustrated in Figure 18. A detailed plot of the southernmost area of survey defined two visible relict wall lines that lie close to the foundations of an old barn outside the survey area.

A substantial archaeological feature seen to the bottom right of Figure 17 has been 'clipped' during the survey. Straight angular lines, interpreted as walls, show one clear return to the north-west. The wall line is enclosing significant archaeological activity, and is sited on a gentle east facing slope. No structure is indicated or visible on the ground at this location.

Interpretation and Conclusions

The geophysical survey revealed significant archaeological anomalies, establishing that substantial archaeological remains exist in close proximity to the helmet find-spot and indeed suggest that it was found within an archaeological site. These results, combined with the limited landscape survey, exhibit a concentration of archaeological activity, in an upland setting. Had the site been assessed purely on the landscape and geophysical survey, it would almost certainly have been interpreted as an Iron Age or Romano-British site. Our subsequent knowledge of the area though, with the finds of the helmet and Roman coins, allows us to categorise the site as Romano-British, though earlier phases may well lie beneath the visible remains.

The possible settlement site would have benefitted from the defensive bank and ditch earthwork seen illustrated in Figure 18 as it is a substantial construction. Likely to represent the land holdings or 'territory' of the builders, this probable Iron-Age earthwork is tentatively the boundary for the proposed settlement site, which may be one of a number within the enclosed area.

The discovery of Roman coins and the helmet at the site would support the idea of trade between the Romans and native peoples. As obvious Roman military earthworks were absent, except for the possible defended entrance, this also supports a Romano-British interpretation. The site does not lie on, or even close to, any known Roman road. The Romano-British interpretation could indicate that territorial defences were bolstered by adding a Roman-type traverse entrance to the outer boundary, allowing access to and from the open fell to the south of the site, resulting in the double earthwork feature at that location.

Interpretation here is offered as a credible theory within the very limited scope of the fieldwork and reporting carried out. The results of this geophysical and topographic survey have served the purpose of drawing attention to a small gap in a vast space of archaeological activity. Further detailed survey work, as well as archaeological intervention across a much larger area, would define and determine the limitations, chronology and typology of the site as a whole, most of which may not have been detected in this area before, and help improve understanding of the interaction between the native Britons and the Romans in the uplands of Cumbria.

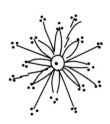

ARCHAEOLOGICAL EVALUATION

Chris Healey

Introduction

Following the geophysical survey, described above, Minerva Heritage Ltd was invited to carry out an archaeological evaluation of the find-spot.It was agreed that three 6m² trenches would be excavated. The first trench (Trench 1) was positioned over the recorded find-spot location (Figures 19 and 21). Two other locations (Trenches 2 and 3) were chosen on the basis that they would investigate features appearing on the geophysical survey results. The purpose of Trench 2 (Figures 20 and 22) was to investigate a potential hut circle, and Trench 3 targeted a possible rectangular building.

The work was carried out in a remote and exposed location, and the project team was both good-humoured and solidly stoic in the face of unrelenting high winds and the occasional fit of cold sideways rain. Mr Robinson, the landowner, helped us to navigate to the find-spot location and the other trenches were positioned using GPS equipment.

Results

Archaeological features identified at the find-spot location (Trench 1) seem to strongly confirm the reported find-spot– a recently-dug and backfilled pit was found at the grid reference provided, and fragments of copper alloy material similar to the helmet were recovered from very close by. These copper-alloy fragments may even have once been part of the helmet; at the time of writing this is yet to be confirmed.

The discovery and subsequent lifting of the helmet had removed any archaeological relationships which might have shed some light on how it came to be here. It was not possible to determine which archaeological layer the helmet was retrieved from. Nevertheless, enough survived to offer some comment. Trench 1 contained a 30mm-thick sequence of deposits, with a stone covering layer sealing a stone-and-earth dump beneath. This could indicate a track surface or a floor foundation, for example, although two sets of stone slabs – found laid onto the bedrock directly underneath this stone and earth layer – might indicate a structural element, which may possibly be related to construction or preparation of a cairn, though other interpretations are possible. At the lowest part of Trench 1 a ditch or gully was identified; we are not certain how – or if – this is connected to the stone layers or the slabs.

The finds recovered from Trench 1 were mostly Roman. These included iron and copper-alloy objects, two coins from the AD 330s, pottery fragments, and animal bones, some of which were burnt. All this confirms in part what the surveys led us to believe: complex Roman remains are present.

The geophysical survey had suggested two superimposed hut circles or the footprints of round-houses, characteristic of some prehistoric and Romano-British settlements, in Trench 2. No features were discovered during the excavation although we did recover an unusually large number of flint

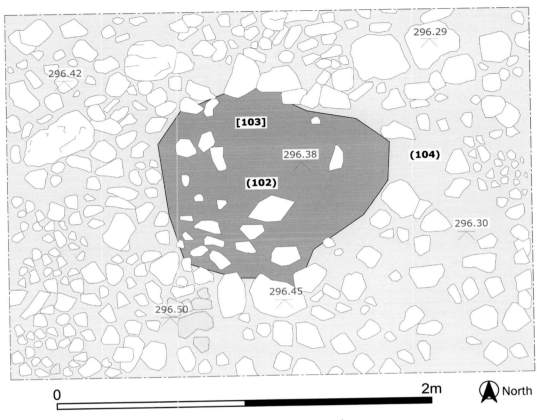

296.29

296.42

[103]

296.38

(104)

(102)

296.30

296.45

296.50

0   2m   North

Figure 19: Plan of Trench 1

and chert fragments which may indicate that hut circles were hereabouts.

Trench 3 was located over what appeared in the geophysical survey to be a rectangular building. We uncovered the edge of a building marked by a wall line consisting of large stones; this was punctuated by postholes. The wall line enclosed a layer of dumped stone which probably represents a floor foundation with a drainage gully beneath it. A single piece of abraded Roman samian ware pottery from the topsoil above the building may suggest that the building is Roman in date.

Post-excavation

A variety of artefacts was recovered on-site during the digging and recording. More artefacts were recovered from bulk samples processed by Museum of London Archaeology.

The artefacts included pieces of what appeared to be part of the helmet. We also recovered other items of Roman metalwork, including the two coins (Figure 23), and a small number of fragments from Roman pottery vessels. The very small quantity of ceramic building material from Trench 1 included a piece of fired clay – this may be daub from a wattle-and-daub wall, perhaps plaster from around a smoke-hole, or maybe a fragment of a hearth.

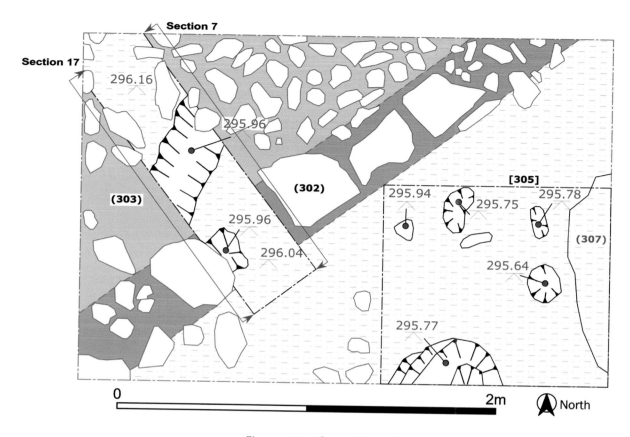

Figure 20: Plan of Trench 2

Over 100 fragments of animal bone were recovered. Some of these had been burnt at high temperature; maybe not deliberately so. None of the bone appeared to have been butchered. The species were mainly cattle, with sheep/goat slightly less prevalent and then horse and other species even less so. Based on this very limited evidence the suggestion is that there was a settlement here with a mixed economy producing meat and milk.

A large number of flint and chert objects dating from the Mesolithic, Neolithic, Bronze Age, and Iron Age were also recovered. These came from the evaluation trenches and from fieldwalking carried out by Stuart Noon, Finds Liaison Officer for Cumbria and Lancashire. The majority of these objects have been dated to between the Bronze Age and the Iron Age. They include cores, scrapers, a blade fragment, a drill, and multi-purpose tools.

Such a dense concentration may indicate that this was a preferred location for prehistoric groups to undertake a wide range of activities. Although we were unable to prove either hut circles or roundhouses at the site, the flints may indicate a prehistoric settlement, or perhaps a natural re-source, which was repeatedly or persistently used by communities over thousands of years.

30

Figure 21: Trench 1

Figure 22: Trench 2

Figure 23: A coin is found

Figure 24: Surveying

Conclusion

This project has confirmed that there are complex Roman and prehistoric remains at and nearby the helmet find-spot. Some of these remains may relate directly to the helmet, although how this was so is now lost to us. The archaeology appears to show that the remains of a Romano-British settlement survive here as below-ground structures, deposits and layers. There is also some kind of, probably unconnected, Bronze Age to Iron Age site. There is also some less-well defined and still-earlier activity present. This matches some of the interpretations put forward by the geophysical and landscape surveys.

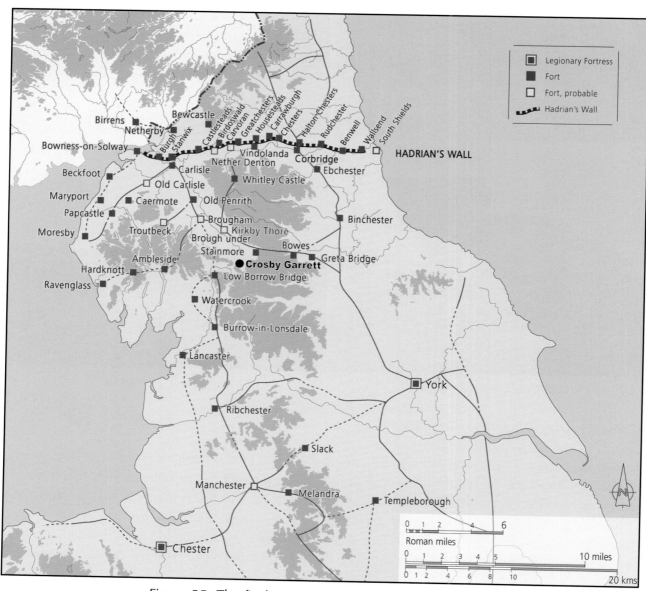

Figure 25: The find-spot on a map of Northern Britain

The map includes the legend:
- Legionary Fortress
- Fort
- Fort, probable
- Hadrian's Wall

HADRIAN'S WALL

Labels: Birrens, Bewcastle, Netherby, Bowness-on-Solway, Burgh, Stanwix, Castlesteads, Birdoswald, Carvoran, Greatchesters, Housesteads, Carrawburgh, Chesters, Halton-Chesters, Rudchester, Benwell, Wallsend, South Shields, Vindolanda, Corbridge, Nether Denton, Carlisle, Ebchester, Beckfoot, Old Carlisle, Whitley Castle, Maryport, Caermote, Old Penrith, Binchester, Papcastle, Brougham, Moresby, Troutbeck, Kirkby Thore, Brough under Stainmore, Bowes, Greta Bridge, Crosby Garrett, Ambleside, Low Borrow Bridge, Hardknott, Ravenglass, Watercrook, Burrow-in-Lonsdale, Lancaster, York, Ribchester, Slack, Manchester, Melandra, Templeborough, Chester

Scale bars: Roman miles (0 1 2 4 6), 10 miles, 20 kms

THE WIDER SETTING

Dot Boughton and David Breeze

Even though, as we have seen, there are several earthworks present in the immediate vicinity of the helmet's find-spot, none have been previously excavated and therefore they cannot help us understand how and why the helmet got to be deposited in this location. There are no known Roman legionary or auxiliary forts nearby, and no surveyed or excavated Romano-British settlements apart from the putative examples discovered through the recent work.

The find-spot of the helmet lies about 10 km east of the main north–south arterial Roman route leading north to Hadrian's Wall, but on the far side of a ridge of fells (Figure 25). The site is closer to the Roman road leading across Stainmore (the modern A66) from Brougham (*Brocavum*) through Kirkby Thore (*Bravoniacum*) to Brough (*Verteris*) and beyond. This road is about 6km distant, and on the far side of the valley of the River Eden. Nevertheless, this is the view which the people living around the find-spot of the helmet would have seen daily – depending on the weather.

Brough is the nearest fort to the find-spot, being about 9km away. Unfortunately, we do not know which unit of the Roman army was based here at the time that the helmet was lost (Bidwell and Hodgson 2009, 60–7; Edwards 2010). A Roman document dating to about AD 400 known as the *Notitia Dignitatum* records the garrison as the *numerus directorum* about which nothing is known. The case for Kirkby Thore is worse as there is no evidence for the regiment based here. Brougham on the other hand has produced evidence that part of the thousand-strong, part-mounted *cohors I Vangionum* was here. This regiment would have contained soldiers who would have been wealthy enough to have worn a helmet such as that found at Crosby Garrett.

Finally, we may turn to the civilian context. It seems highly likely that this area was part of the territory of the Carvetii, a tribe which appears to have occupied the Eden Valley, probably with its main city at Carlisle (Breeze 2008; Higham and Jones 1985). The tribe had been awarded self-governing rights by the Romans by the 3rd century at the latest.

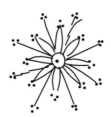

THE INTERNATIONAL CONTEXT
M C Bishop and J C N Coulston

Roman cavalry

During the first two-and-a-half centuries of the Roman occupation of Britain, the major cavalry component of the army was divided between two types of auxiliary unit. Most prestigious were the fully mounted units (alae), known as quingenariae (512 men and horses in 16 turmae) or milliariae (768 men and horses in 24 turmae). Below these were the part-mounted units (cohortes equitatae), with a mixture of infantry and cavalry, similarly called quingenariae (480 infantry/128 cavalry in 6 centuries and 4 turmae) and milliariae (800 infantry/256 cavalry in 10 centuries and 8 turmae). The turma or troop was thus the basic mounted sub-unit for all of these types of unit and it comprised around 30 men and their horses, together with an officer (the decurio) and standard-bearer (signifer).

Auxiliary troops were raised from the provincial peoples of the Empire. Like legionaries, they were volunteers and received pay for their service, but unlike the men of the legions, they were not Roman citizens (at least, not until the grant of universal citizenship made under the Emperor Caracalla in AD 212). Instead, they received a grant of citizenship upon completion of 25 years' service. All Roman soldiers were expected to pay for their own kit and rations, cavalrymen having to provide for both themselves and their horse (so they were paid more than auxiliary infantry).

The original owner (or owners: inscriptions on other objects sometimes reveal more than one) of the Crosby Garrett helmet would have had to provide himself with battle equipment as well as his sports gear, since the two served different purposes. The Roman army did not have 'parade' equipment as such, and formal parades (when they were paid three times a year or when they were addressed by the provincial governor and, on extremely rare occasions, even the emperor) would see them turn out in their full battle array, without any leather covers on shields or helmets, with crests and plumes attached, and with everything that could be polished gleaming (Bishop 1990). Face-mask, or sports helmets were not part of such parades, for they had a different function.

Face-mask helmets

Helmets with face masks were first used during the 4th century BC (the Hellenistic period, from the time of Alexander the Great), but the earliest certain finds from the Roman era come from the 1st century AD, with face-mask visors fitted to regular battle helmets. The most notable example of this type was excavated from the battlefield site of Kalkriese (Germany) (Figure 26), thought to be part of the AD 9 debacle in the Teutoburg Forest, where three legions led by Quinctilius Varus were almost completely wiped out by Germanic tribesmen. The purpose of such visors was probably as much psychological (depersonalising the wearer) as protective, but by the third decade of the 1st century AD, the first example occurs of a dateable cavalry sports helmet with a face mask in a grave at Chassenard (France) (Figure 27).

Figure 26: The Kalkriese mask
(© akg-images/Kalkriese Museum)

Figure 27: The Chassenard face mask
(after Déchelette)

Face-mask helmets found at Nijmegen (Netherlands) and dating to the second half of the 1st century AD show the use of what can only be described as hair-nets to simulate real hair. Cavalry battle helmets frequently bore moulded representations of human hair, usually accompanied by a laurel wreath, and this device is echoed on the masks of 'sports' helmets like those from Ribchester (Lancashire) (Figure 28) and Leiden-Matilo (Netherlands) (Figure 29). The Ribchester helmet was found with a hoard of other material, including items of cavalry equipment, that had been concealed within a box, probably during the latter part of the 1st or early years of the 2nd century AD.

Sports helmets reached the zenith of their development in the 3rd century AD, by which time they had become more ambitious in both their forms and their detailing, typified by the depiction of the iris and pupil within the eye opening. This feature can be seen on helmets from Nola (Italy) (Figure 30), Eining (Figure 31), and Straubing (both Germany) and it is also found on the Crosby Garrett helmet. Face-mask helmets of this later period had polarised into depictions of male and female characters, reflecting the roles of Greek and Amazon in the *hippika gymnasia* (see below), whilst a further group depicted androgynous youths, evidently intended as Trojans. Several hoards that included such helmets are known from Continental Europe, most notable amongst which are those from Eining and Straubing. Deposited during the dismantling of installations in the 3rd century AD, these contained a number of face-mask helmet components which provide parallels for the Crosby Garrett example and help to date it. A female face type is found on the face mask from Eining, marked by piles of luxurious curls surrounding the face and rising to a peak, whilst the eye-

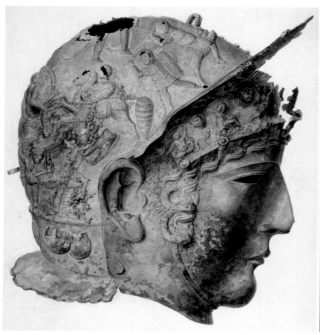

Figure 28: The Ribchester helmet
(© The Society of Antiquaries of London)

Figure 29: The Leiden-Matilo helmet mask
(© Rijksmuseum van Oudheden, Leiden)

Figure 30: The Nola helmet
(© Trustees of the British Museum)

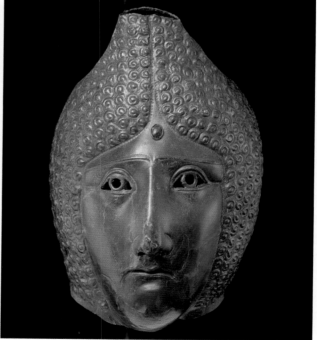

Figure 31: Eining 'Amazon' helmet
(© Archäologische Staatssammlung München,
M. Eberlein)

Figure 32: The Vindolanda griffin (© Vindolanda Trust; drawing: Mark Hoyle)

brows are extremely fine. In the middle of the forehead is a blue glass gem within a raised setting. Two similar face masks occur in another hoard from a villa 3km from the fort at Straubing. All three share the same features of luxurious curls surrounding the face, rising to a peak and with a forehead jewel. This type of helmet is, rather obviously, known as the 'Female' type. Although these have certain features in common with the Crosby Garrett face mask, a helmet bowl in the Museum of Fine Arts in Boston (USA) provides a close parallel for the Phrygian cap motif (James forthcoming).

Other details of the Crosby Garrett helmet can be paralleled elsewhere. The voluted band passing around the rear of the bowl is reminiscent of a similar raised ridge on a battle helmet from Heddernheim (Germany). The cast griffin ornament on top of the Phrygian cap was subsequently paralleled by the find of a similar (but not identical) piece from Vindolanda (Northumberland), co-incidentally found outside the 3rd century fort in 2010 (Figure 32). The Vindolanda object differs in detail (it lacks the loops and its base is not convex like that on the Crosby Garrett helmet) but is similar in size. Components of helmets from across the Empire could often bear more than a passing resemblance, a result of troop movements and the dissemination of tastes. The fact that the Ribchester helmet may have been associated with a sphinx ornament, now lost and probably from a second helmet, suggests that the Crosby Garrett ornament may not have been a unique addition (Jackson 2010; Breeze and Edwards 2012). An unprovenanced helmet in a private collection, of a similar type to that from Ribchester, features two projecting attachments with loops that may have fulfilled a similar function to the loops on the Crosby Garrett griffin (Fischer 2012, Abb.332). This appears to support the notion that the griffin may have been related to a method of crest or plume attachment.

At the same time as this kind of effeminate and female forms of face mask was in use, another type depicted a distinctly masculine appearance. This latter form had bushy eyebrows, more pronounced brow ridges, and centrally parted locks of hair. These are so reminiscent of portraits of Alexander the Great that they have been named the 'Alexander' type (Figure 33). It may be no co-

Figure 33: Straß-Moos 'Alexander' helmet (© Archäologische Staatssammlung München, S Mulzer)

Figure 34: Hellenistic 'Phrygian' helmet with face-mask cheek-pieces (© J C N Coulston)

incidence that helmets with the bowl in the form of a Phrygian cap were also worn by Macedonian cavalry at the time of Alexander, and these are now known as 'Phrygian' helmets (Figure 34) (Waurick 1988). These same Hellenistic helmets were amongst the first to evolve their cheekpieces into a form of face mask (Robinson 1975).

It is important to remember that not every cavalryman in the army will have had both battle and 'sports' equipment. Arrian wrote that only certain men (possibly officers and the best horsemen; the text is unclear on this point) wore face-mask helmets 'to attract the attention of onlookers'. This makes the survival of such helmets all the more remarkable. A small number of hoards of 'sports' equipment, including those from Straubing and Eining, date to the unrest of the 3rd century AD, when there were barbarian incursions into the Empire. These only serve to underline the rarity of these finds. The regard in which the face-mask helmets was held is similarly indicated by elite burials of the late 1st/early 2nd century AD at Nawa (Syria) and Čatalka (Bulgaria), which included such helmets alongside regular battle gear (Garbsch 1978, 61–2 and 67). This reflects the earlier practice of interring helmets with an emphasis on masked designs, seen in Scythian, Thracian, and Macedonian funerary contexts. Accordingly, it has been suggested that these helmets belonged to men who had served as the commanders of auxiliary or allied cavalry units.

Cavalrymen evidently took great pride in their appearance, illustrated by their preference for having themselves depicted on gravestones (Schleiermacher 1984). An example belonging to a trooper of *ala Augusta* called Insus, brandishing the severed head of a barbarian opponent, was excavated outside the fort at Lancaster (Bull 2007). The gravestone of the standard bearer Flavinus,

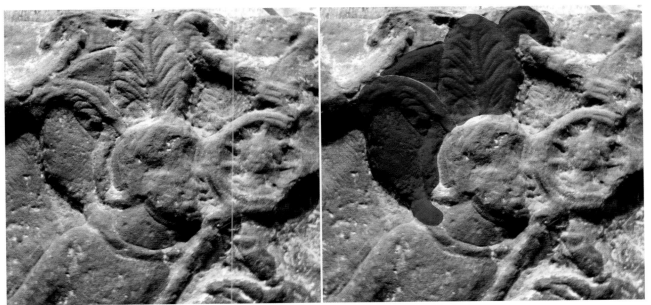

Figure 35: Detail of the tombstone of Flavinus in Hexham Abbey indicating (right) his hair crest (blue) and plumes (red) (© M C Bishop)

found built into Hexham Abbey, shows him with a full front-to-back crest and side plumes on his helmet (Figure 35). Although it is frequently suggested that Flavinus is shown wearing a face-mask helmet, this is a difficult assertion to prove, since his stone is both fairly crudely sculpted and damaged.

Cavalry sports helmets could be manufactured from copper alloy or iron. They were well within the capabilities of most experienced craftsmen in military workshops and a ferrous face-mask from the Augustan fort at Haltern (Germany) was found corroded to an anvil. Surface analysis of the Crosby Garrett helmet was carried out with a portable X-ray fluorescence spectrometer (Fillery-Travis 2011). Such machines can produce inaccurate results for various reasons (including the presence of intrusive corrosion products, changes in the alloy due to 'sweating' over time, and the presence of surface tinning and solder). Nevertheless, the readings provide a broad indication of the type of alloy used and the readings – indicative of a tin brass – compare well with a face-mask helmet of the same period from Weißenburg (Germany) (Born and Junkelmann 1997). Such an alloy would be well-suited for working complex, three-dimensional decoration.

The end seems to have come suddenly for cavalry 'sports' equipment. Following Diocletian's reforms of the army at the end of the 3rd and beginning of the 4th century, face-mask helmets appear to have disappeared completely out of Roman military use.

The *hippika gymnasia*

The Roman writer Flavius Arrianus (or Arrian), one of the Emperor Hadrian's governors, as well as a personal friend, wrote a treatise in Greek on warfare. This was heavily influenced by his hero, the historian Xenophon, but at the same time described contemporary practice in some areas. Within this

Figure 36: Reconstruction of the Hippika Gymnasia *(© akg-images / Peter Connolly)*

Technē Taktika, he included a section on the Roman cavalry training exercises which he called the *hippika gymnasia* (DeVoto 1993; Hyland 1993). The Greek term, which is still used to describe the exercises, was probably just a literal translation of an original Latin phrase which has not survived, but may have been something like *exercitatio equestris* (or 'cavalry training'). Indeed, there is an inscription (*RIB* 978) from Netherby (in Cumbria, just north of Hadrian's Wall) marking the reconstruction of a *basilica equestris exercitatoria* or cavalry training hall.

Arrian stressed that the manoeuvres he described were largely Celtic in origin and they in fact use mainly Celtic terminology for two reasons. The first is that the majority of Roman auxiliary cavalry were recruited from northern peoples (Gauls, Germans, Thracians). Secondly, these peoples practised a form of mounted warfare using spears, javelins and shields, often in combination with long swords, which required further exploration because it was little represented in the traditional *taktika* literary genre in which Arrian was working. He described a sequence of manoeuvres which he called the *Testudo* (literally Tortoise), the *Petrinos*, the Cantabrian Circle, the *Touloutegon*, and the *Hodoiporikon*. These were performed by two *turmae* upon the *campus* or exercise ground associated with a fort (see below) and in front of a group of spectators upon a *tribunal* (Figure 36).

The *Testudo* consisted of one team of riders lining up and, facing backwards, covering both themselves and their horses with their shields. The other team meanwhile rode off ready to attack them. Two men in armour (most were evidently just wearing tunics) placed themselves further back, closer to their opponents, in order to act as human targets. Now the functional purpose of

Arrian on face-mask helmets

'2. The riders themselves, according to rank or because they distinguish themselves in horse-manship, set off with golden helmets of iron or bronze, in order to attract the attention of onlookers by this means. 3. Unlike battle helmets, these defend not only the head and cheeks but, conforming to the faces of the riders, have openings for the eyes which do not hinder the vision and yet offer protection. 4. Crests of yellow hair, which have no function other than to act as decoration, hang down from the helmets. These flutter as the horse trots or if a light breeze blows, and offer a fine spectacle.'

Arrian, *Technē taktika* 34

face-mask helmets becomes apparent. The danger inherent in this was also acknowledged by the horses' heads being protected with chamfrons which covered their face and ears (Figures 36–8). The horses were also provided with openwork metal eye-guards, either integral with the chamfron or attached separately, according to the type used.

The opposing team now rode past and attempted to hit those outlying men with dummy javelins. This is the point at which another manoeuvre was undertaken by the defending team, whereby some members rode out and attempted to cast their own dummy javelins at their attackers as they went past, crossing their path as they did so. This was called the *Petrinos* in Celtic.

The Cantabrian Circle saw the two teams riding in opposing circles and, at the point where they almost touched, exchanging dummy javelins whilst defending themselves with their shields.

Then, after some more javelin throwing (including a turning throw, known in Greek as *xynema*), the cavalry would demonstrate the *Touloutegon*, where the riders defended themselves from an attack from the rear using both spears and drawn swords.

The final task for the cavalrymen was to mount, fully armoured, onto a galloping horse, known as *Hodoiporikon* (or 'the itinerary'). The Late Roman writer Vegetius stressed the importance of being able to vault onto a horse (Milner 1996, 18). Arrian noted that a number of 'barbarian' man-oeuvres were introduced by Hadrian, emulating the Parthian and Armenian mounted archers (renowned for loosing arrows backwards whilst retreating, the so-called 'Parthian shot') and the Celtic and Sarmatian lance-armed troopers.

Each of these evolutions seems to have been derived or adapted from a regular combat tactic. Not all of Rome's enemies were equally sophisticated, and derisory comments about British cavalry preserved in one of the writing tablets found at the fort of Vindolanda (Northumberland) suggest that 'Celtic' cavalry were not all the same (*Tab. Vindol.* II.164).

The manoeuvres described are clearly a ritualised form of training for both men and horses, with units divided into competing teams. Both horses and riders were afforded some protection, since even practice javelins could potentially cause serious injury. Horses had chamfrons to protect their faces, complete with openwork eyepieces, so that the horse could see where it was going. The men wore brightly coloured Cimmerian tunics and, Arrian tells us, some of the more distinguished

Figure 37: Leather chamfron from Newstead (© Trustees of the National Museums of Scotland)

and/or accomplished riders wore face-mask helmets. It is in this context that differentiation between the competitors could be effected by means of their equipment, and most notably their face-mask helmets.

The cavalry exercises described in such detail by Arrian are again briefly referred to in the surviving text of a large inscription recording the Emperor Hadrian's address to his African army. There, both the cavalry of the *alae* and their colleagues in the *cohortes equitatae* are found undertaking the same tasks. As an aside, the Emperor acknowledged that the latter were not expected to match the former in terms of appearance and performance.

The origin of the *hippika gymnasia* may ultimately lie with what was known as the Troy Game (*lusus Troiae*), where young members of the nobility split into teams (in this case three of them), dressed up as Greeks and Trojans, and performed a series of manoeuvres (Ross 2007). With masked helmets, the teams were clearly distinguished as idealised Greek males (*epheboi*) and as evidently female Amazons, a tribe of unnaturally warlike women who also partook in the Trojan War. Two 3rd-century AD shields from Dura-Europos (Syria) also make these connections by depicting scenes from the Trojan War and of combat between Greeks and Amazons (*Amazonomachia*). One depicts the Amazons (with piled-up hair) performing the 'Parthian shot' against armoured Greeks whilst the other shows Trojans (wearing Phrygian caps) inspecting the Trojan Horse (James 2004, 176–9 with Plates 6–7). Coincidentally, one of the units in garrison at Dura was the part-mounted *cohors XX Palmyrenorum*, who would presumably have been fully conversant in the *hippika gymnasia*. This association of Trojans with the Phrygian cap is brought full circle by a 4th-century mosaic from Low Ham (Somerset) which shows a naked Dido embracing her lover, the Phrygian-cap-wearing Aeneas, son of the last king of Troy (Cosh and Neal 2007, 254–6).

The failure of cavalry sports equipment to survive the Diocletianic army reforms implies that the *hippika gymnasia* was no longer practised in the 4th century AD. This is unsurprising, since the troops forming the cavalry were changing and the long Celtic tradition was broken in favour of Germanic, Persian, and Asiatic steppe horse-borne cultures.

Exercise grounds

Although it is common to speak of 'parade grounds', in truth the Romans would not have recognised the concept. They referred to exercise or training grounds (*campi exercitatoriae*). Every fort will have had one, but comparatively few are known. Legionary examples (Bishop 2013, 36) are known out-with the fortresses at Caerleon (Gwent), Mirebeau (France), and Lambaesis (Algeria) and these may have been used by their associated cavalry units (the *legio II Augusta* at Caerleon seems to have been brigaded together with *ala I Thracum*). *Campi* are known outside the Praetorian Camp in Rome and next to the fort of the *equites singulares Augusti* (Coulston 2000, Fig. 5.1). Auxiliary exercise grounds are rarer, but one (140m by 80m) is known outside the fort at Hardknott (Cumbria), although this site was occupied by an auxiliary infantry unit so is not necessarily directly comparable with a cavalry *campus* (Bidwell *et al.* 1999, 29). At Maryport, where part-mounted units were based, a likely exercise ground, about 90m square, was long known next to Pudding Pie Hill, thought to be its *tribunal* (Daniels 1978, 277). Hadrian even hints that the *campi* of an *ala* and a *cohors equitata* differed in size (see boxout). Nevertheless, we have some idea of what an exercise ground was like.

Training soldiers with sword and shield against the fencing-post (*palus*) was a prime purpose of the exercise ground, together with development of missile skills (javelins, bows, stones), and the same must have been as true for cavalrymen as for infantrymen (Coulston 1998). There is also evidence for pride in the exercise of horse archery, as displayed on the gravestone of Acrabanis from Győr (Hungary), which depicts the deceased riding at full gallop at a target with three arrows already projecting from it. Another gravestone from Walbersdorf (Austria), shows a horseman, again at full gallop, who has shot two barbarians and already has a third arrow nocked. These are skills very similar to those described in later Egyptian Mamluk archery treatises, and still displayed today in the Japanese *yabusame*. In the same way that Hadrian was treated to displays of marksmanship in North Africa (see boxout), so another (unnamed) cavalryman claimed on an inscription to have swum across the River Danube in full equipment with his horse, then shot an arrow in the air and hit it with a second, all under the emperor's watchful gaze (Campbell 1994, 35).

The cavalry training hall at Netherby mentioned above could have been used for exercising horses in bad weather, as advised by Vegetius (Milner 1993, 18 and 57–9) but it is extremely unlikely that the *hippika gymnasia* evolutions described by Arrian could be performed in their entirety indoors. It is more likely that the sort of horse control illustrated on some tombstones, using long reins, could have been practised here along with some simple riding manoeuvres.

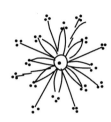

BIBLIOGRAPHY

Bishop, M C 1990: 'On parade: status, display, and morale in the Roman army' in *Akten der 14. Internationalen Limeskongresses in Bad Deutsch-Altenburg/Carnuntum, 14.–21. September 1986*, Römische Limes in Österreich Sonderband, Vienna, 21–30

Bidwell, P and Hogson, N 2009: *The Roman Army in Northern England*, South Shields

Bidwell, P, Snape, M, and Croom, A 1999: *Hardknott Roman Fort, Cumbria*, Kendal

Bishop, M C 2013: *Handbook to Roman Legionary Fortresses*, Barnsley

Born, H and Junkelmann, M 1997: *Römische Kampf- und Turnierrüstungen*, Sammlung Axel Guttmann, Bd. **6**, Berlin

Breeze, D J 2008: 'Civil government in the North: the Carvetii, Brigantes and Rome', *Transactions of the Cumberland and Westmorland Archaeological and Antiquarian Society* 3rd series, **8**, 63–72

Breeze, D J 2012: 'The Roman military occupation of Northern England', *Transactions of the Cumberland and Westmorland Archaeological and Antiquarian Society* 3rd series, **11**, 113–36

Breeze, D J and Edwards, B J N 2012 'The sphinx crest in the Ribchester hoard', *Antiquaries Journal* **92**, 65–9

Bull, S 2007: *Triumphant Rider: The Lancaster Roman Cavalry Tombstone*, Lancaster

Campbell, J B 1994: *The Roman Army, 31 BC–AD 337: A Sourcebook*, London

Clark, A 2001: *Seeing Beneath the Soil: Prospecting Methods in Archaeology*, London

Cosh, S R and Neal, D S 2007: *Roman Mosaics of Britain: South-West Britain*, London

Coulston, J C N 1998: 'Gladiators and soldiers: personnel and equipment in *ludus* and *castra*', *Journal of Roman Military Equipment Studies* **9**, 1–17

Coulston, J C N 2000: 'Armed and belted men: the soldiery in imperial Rome', in Coulston, J C N and Dodge, H (eds), *Ancient Rome: the Archaeology of the Eternal City*, Oxford University School of Archaeology Monograph **54**, Oxford, 76–118

Cunliffe, B W 1995: *English Heritage Book of Iron Age Britain*, London

Daniels, C (ed) 1978: *Handbook to the Roman Wall, by J Collingwood Bruce*, ed 13, Newcastle upon Tyne

DeVoto, J G 1993: *Flavius Arrianus* Technē taktika *and* Ektaxis kata Alanōn *(The Expedition Against the Alans)*, Chicago

Ekserdjian, D 2012: entry no 42, in Ekserdjian, D (ed.), *Bronze*, London, 136–7 and 260

Fillery-Travis, R, 2011: 'Report on the XRF analysis of the Crosby Garrett Helmet', in Worrell and Pearce 2011, 405

Fischer, T 2012: *Die Armee der Caesaren. Archäologie und Geschichte*, Regensburg

Garbsch, J 1978: *Römische Paraderüstungen*, München

Higham, N and Jones, B 1985: *The Carvetii*, Stroud

Hyland, A 1993: *Training the Roman Cavalry from Arrian's Ars Tactica*, Stroud

Jackson, R 2010: *Roman Cavalry Sports Helmet from Crosby Garrett, Cumbria*, unpublished report

James, S 2004: *Excavations at Dura-Europos Final Report VII, the Arms and Armour and Other Military Equipment*, London

James, S. forthcoming: 'The Boston helmet: a preliminary account of a Parthian/Roman-era artefact in the Museum of Fine Arts', in *Life in the Limes*

Jones, D M (ed) 2008: *Geophysical Survey in Archaeological Field Evaluation*, Research and Professional Services Guidance No 1, 2nd Edition, Swindon

Kohlert, M 1978: 'Typologie und Chronologie der Gesichtsmasken', in Garbsch 1978, 19–28

Milner, N P 1996: *Vegetius: Epitome of Military Science*, ed 2, Liverpool

Noon, S 2011: *Written Scheme of Investigation: Crosby Garrett*, Portable Antiquities Scheme: Unpublished Report Number WSI 1.001–2

Robinson, H R 1975: *The Armour of Imperial Rome*, London

Ross, D 2007: *Virgil's Aeneid: A Reader's Guide*, London

Schleiermacher, M 1984: *Römische Reitergrabsteine. Die kaiserzeitlichen Reliefs des triumphierenden Reiters*, Bonn

Shotter, D C A 1996: *The Roman Frontier in Britain: Hadrian's Wall, the Antonine Wall and Roman Policy in the North*, Oxford

Shotter, D C A 1997: *Romans and Britons in North-West England*, Lancaster

Speidel, M 2006: *Emperor Hadrian's Speeches to the African Army – a New Text*, Mainz

Waurick, G 1988: 'Römische Helme' in A. Bottini *et al.*, *Antike Helme*, RGZM Monograph **14**, Mainz, 327–538

Worrell, S, Jackson, R, Mackay, A, Bland, R and Pitts, M 2011: 'The Crosby Garrett Roman Helmet', *British Archaeology* **116**, 20–7

Worrell, S, and Pearce, J, 2011: 'Finds reported under the Portable Antiquities Scheme', *Britannia* **42**, 399–437

ACKNOWLEDGEMENTS

We are grateful to Mr Eric Robinson for allowing access to his land to undertake the geophysical survey and the excavation. Funding for the geophysical survey and excavation was provided by the Portable Antiquities Scheme. Mark Brennand, Andrew Mackay, Stuart Noon and Tim Padley provided advice in relation to the geophysical survey and subsequent excavation.

We should like to thank the following for help in preparing this booklet: Tom Hazenberg of Hazenberg Archaeologie for permission to use the image of the Leiden-Matilo face mask; Duncan Campbell for help interpreting the text of Arrian; Andrew Birley for details of, and permission to publish, the Vindolanda griffin; Holger von Grawert for advice and top-notch intel; Prof Tom Fischer and Ralph Jackson for timely interventions; and David Sim for metallurgical and technical advice. Prof Michael Speidel kindly allowed us to use his translations of the Lambaesis inscriptions. Hilary Wade, Tim Padley, and Michelle Wiggins helped collect material for the booklet and the following institutions and individuals kindly assisted with the provision of illustrations: akg-images/Estate of Peter Connolly; akg-images/Kalkriese Museum; Archäologische Staatssammlung München; Christie's; Johnny Shumate; Rijksmuseum van Oudheden, Leiden; The Society of Antiquaries of London; The Trustees of the British Museum; The Trustees of the National Museums of Scotland; and The Vindolanda Trust.

CONTRIBUTORS

M C Bishop	Editor, *Journal of Roman Military Equipment Studies*
Dot Boughton	Finds Liaison Officer for Lancashire and Cumbria; Department of Portable Antiquities and Treasure, The British Museum, London; Tullie House Museum & Art Gallery, Tullie House, Carlisle
Darren Bradbury	Darren Bradbury Ltd
David J Breeze	President, Cumberland and Westmorland Antiquarian and Archaeological Society
J C N Coulston	School of Classics, University of St Andrews
David Ekserdjian	Professor of History of Art and Film, University of Leicester
Mark Graham	Grampus Heritage and Training Ltd
Chris Healey	Minerva Heritage Ltd
Patricia Shaw	Grampus Heritage and Training Ltd

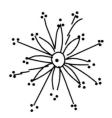

Figure 38: Roman cavalryman performing the hippika gymnasia *wearing the Crosby Garrett helmet (© Johnny Shumate)*